Mapping Global Issues

Infectious Diseases

Mapping Global Issues

Infectious Diseases

Anne Rooney

A⁺

Smart Apple Media

Published in the United States by Smart Apple Media
PO Box 3263, Mankato, Minnesota 56002

Copyright © 2012 Arcturus Publishing Limited

This book has been published in cooperation with Arcturus Publishing Limited.

Series concept: Alex Woolf   Editor and picture researcher: Alex Woolf
Designer: Jane Hawkins   Map illustrator: Stefan Chabluk

Library of Congress Cataloging-in-Publication Data
Rooney, Anne.
Infectious diseases / Anne Rooney.
p. cm.—(Mapping global issues)
 Summary: "Describes the history of pandemics and infectious diseases, how they spread and are tracked,
 and ways we can fight and prevent pandemics. Includes charts and maps"—Provided by publisher.
Includes index.
ISBN 978-1-59920-510-6 (library binding)
1. Communicable diseases—Juvenile literature. I. Title.
RC112.R58 2012
616.9—dc22
                        2011000249

Picture credits
Centers for Disease Control: 41 (James Gathany).
Corbis: 11 (Peter Turnley), 17 (Bettmann), 22 (Patrick Robert/Sygma), 25 (Bettmann), 26 (Chaiwat Subprasom/Reuters), 34 (Howard Davies).
Shutterstock: 7 (Andrey Shadrin), 37 (Michael Taylor).

Cover picture: A child is vaccinated against the H1N1 influenza virus in a sports hall in Schiedam, the Netherlands.

Map sources
9: Centers for Disease Control and Prevention; 18: Rogers, Randolph. The Global Spread of Malaria in a Future, Warmer World. Science (2000; 1763-1766); 21: Based on data from UNAIDS 2008 global report; 28: Based on data from World Health Organization, 2003; 31: C F Cheffins, 1854 in On the Mode of Communication of Cholera by John Snow (John Churchill, 1855); 39: World Health Organization, 2010; 42–43: World Health Organization, 2003.

Printed at CT, China.
SL001635US

PO1038
08-2011

9 8 7 6 5 4 3 2 1

Contents

Understanding Infectious Diseases

Infectious diseases have plagued humans for thousands of years and continue to kill millions of people every year. Fear of disease has driven developments in science as people have struggled to understand and combat the infections that afflict them. The challenge remains today with old and new diseases threatening people around the world.

Out of the Blue

Disease may strike individuals randomly, sweep through a community in an epidemic, or follow in the wake of other catastrophes. Often, there is no clear trigger for an outbreak of disease. It can appear to come from nowhere, infecting a community, a whole country, or even the entire world. Many diseases lie dormant in a community for years or even centuries before flaring up with no apparent cause. This can happen if the organism causing the disease changes by mutation and people in the area have no immunity to the new form. New diseases have been introduced by explorers or invaders. Disease can spread very quickly when the local population has no immunity, and the effects can be disastrous.

After natural disasters such as floods and earthquakes, infectious diseases quickly take hold among survivors and can spread very rapidly, often increasing the death toll far beyond that caused by the original event.

Throughout history, more people have been killed by disease and infection during wars than have died in combat. Soldiers usually live in poor, cramped conditions that make it very easy for diseases to spread. Typhus and cholera have afflicted armies for thousands of years. The bacteria multiplies

FACTS and FIGURES

CURRENT RATES OF INFECTION

DISEASE	CASES/DEATHS PER YEAR
Bubonic plague	2,118 cases (2003)
Cholera	100,000–120,000 cases (2010)
Malaria	863,000 deaths (2008)
AIDS	2 million deaths (2010)
Yellow fever	200,000 cases (2009) 30,000 deaths (2009)
Measles	164,000 deaths (2008)

Source: World Health Organization

quickly in conditions where hygiene is poor and water is often polluted with human waste.

From Slight Sniffles to Instant Death

Not all infectious diseases are deadly. Minor infections such as colds can also spread quickly through a group. However, some diseases that cause only minor illness in most people can be deadly for others. For many people, influenza, or flu, causes an unpleasant and inconvenient bout of illness that lasts only a few days. But for some people, who are already weakened by another illness, it can be deadly. The same is true of diseases such as mumps, chicken pox, and rubella, which used to be common childhood infections before routine vaccinations. Most children recovered quickly, but some suffered lasting disability or even died. Suppressing infectious diseases—even apparently mild diseases—is an important way of safeguarding entire populations.

Coughing and sneezing into a handkerchief or tissue is a simple way of helping to prevent the spread of disease.

How Disease Spreads

Most infectious diseases are caused by microorganisms—bacteria, viruses, fungi, or protozoa. These can spread from person to person in different ways. Bacteria can be transferred through the air, through drinking water, or by direct contact. Some illnesses cause people to cough or sneeze, sending tiny droplets into the air, which may be carrying disease-causing microorganisms. These may infect someone else if they are breathed in, ingested, or land on an open wound or a permeable membrane such as the surface of the eye.

Other infections are carried by water. Bacteria or protozoa may be carried into the water supply in the excrement or urine of an infected person. Anyone drinking or bathing in that water or using it to wash or prepare food is at risk of catching the disease.

Some diseases are carried in body fluids, such as blood, saliva, and semen. Diseases may be transferred during sex or by sharing food. They also may be carried from one person to another by insects that bite.

An organism that carries a disease between people is called a transmission vector. Examples are the very tiny parasites that live in the guts of some mosquitoes and fleas and carry human diseases between people when the insect bites a host.

Spreading Far and Wide

A disease is considered endemic if it exists naturally in a community at some level and may cause occasional outbreaks or affect a few people. Often, people have some resistance or immunity to endemic diseases because they have been exposed to the disease in the past.

If a disease spreads to many people, it causes an epidemic. When more people become ill from the disease than usual, it may become a medical emergency. An endemic disease can become epidemic if more people are vulnerable to the disease than usual—perhaps because they are weakened by hunger or cold or live in poor conditions. To survive, a disease needs a reservoir of people or other hosts in which it continues to live between larger outbreaks. Sometimes, the disease survives in animals. For example, plague survives in rodents between human epidemics.

CASE STUDY

RYAN WHITE

A U.S. teenager, Ryan White suffered from hemophilia, a condition that prevents blood from clotting. He required medicines made from donated blood and became infected with Human Immunodeficiency Virus from contaminated blood products in 1984. White became a spokesman for HIV research and public education. White died in 1990. Researchers are still looking for a cure for HIV.

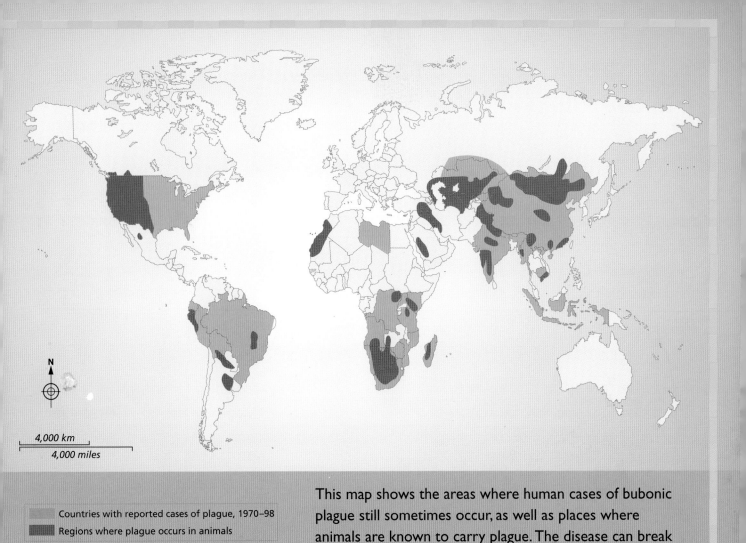

4,000 km

4,000 miles

This map shows the areas where human cases of bubonic plague still sometimes occur, as well as places where animals are known to carry plague. The disease can break out of these animal reservoirs and cause human epidemics.

A new disease often causes an epidemic because the population has no resistance to it. If an outbreak of disease spreads over a very wide area, such as a continent or the entire world, it is known as a pandemic.

Unusual Transmission

A few diseases are spread by unusual methods. The disease kuru, which first appeared in Papua New Guinea in the 1950s, is caused by prions—very tiny particles of protein that can reproduce themselves.

Prions are found in the brain and nervous tissue of people infected with kuru. Prions were passed between people in the Fore tribe who had a burial custom that involved relatives eating the brains of the person who had died. However, prions are not destroyed by heat. Prions also cause variant CJD (Creutzfeld-Jacob disease), a fatal condition that people can develop after eating meat from cattle with BSE (bovine spongiform encephalitis). These diseases slowly destroy the brains of sufferers.

CHOLERA IN SOMALIA

The spread of cholera is hard to prevent when people are living in congested conditions and don't have enough clean water or adequate sanitation. There is an urgent need to allocate more land ... to house and help refugees from Somalia.

Kellie Leeson, International
Rescue Committee, Somalia

How Far and How Fast?

The rate of spread of a disease, and the number of people it will affect, depend on several factors. A disease is very contagious if it is easily transferred between people. If many people exposed to a disease catch it, the disease is said to have a high morbidity rate.

The incubation period is the time it takes for someone who has caught a disease to begin showing symptoms and feeling ill. Diseases spread more easily if they can be passed on before sufferers feel unwell, because sick people tend to have less contact with other people.

If a disease kills a large proportion of the people who catch it, it is said to have a high mortality rate. If people fall ill and die quickly, they have less chance to pass the disease on to other people. In addition, if a disease kills everyone who catches it, there is no reservoir left in which the bacteria or virus can survive between epidemics. This may be why some deadly diseases of the past seem to have died out and never recurred.

For a disease to spread and survive successfully, it needs a long incubation period to be capable of transmission during the incubation period and not kill all of its victims.

Survivors of a disease usually have immunity. However, as children are born without immunity, the disease can surface again. A disease may recur more quickly if it changes, bypassing the immunity people have developed.

Making it Easy for Disease

People living in overcrowded conditions with poor hygiene often have compromised health. They are more likely to fall ill and more likely to die or be seriously affected by disease. Epidemics affect people who live in poverty or run-down areas more severly.

Cholera affects refugees in a camp in Rwanda. Disease spreads quickly when people live close together and have limited access to clean water. Rehydration packs, such as the one held by the child, are a vital tool in combating cholera.

Infectious Diseases in the Past

Tens of thousands of years ago, when people lived in very small groups, infectious diseases were probably rare. As we formed societies, it became possible for diseases to pass easily from one person to another in a larger group. As a range of human diseases appeared, our battle against infection began.

The First Infections

As people began farming animals and living in close proximity to them, some bacteria and viruses that previously infected animals developed forms that specifically targeted people. Flu, for example, came to people first from pigs and poultry. Tuberculosis (TB) probably first came from cattle. This animal-to-human path remains open. New strains of flu still cross to humans from pigs and poultry, and variant CJD came about when people ate brain and nerve tissue from beef infected with BSE.

Medical anthropologists and historians study the diseases that affected our ancestors. Early writings mention diseases and epidemics that ravaged ancient societies in Europe and Asia, and there is physical evidence of disease in the form of human remains. Evidence collected from Egyptian mummies shows that some diseases of today had afflicted ancient Egyptians and likely included polio, smallpox, plague, tuberculosis, and malaria.

Early Plagues and Epidemics

The earliest known epidemic occurred in the eleventh century BC among the Philistines in Ashdod (now Israel). It may have been typhoid or bubonic plague. Around 500 BC, a terrible plague that still cannot be identified killed a large number of inhabitants of Athens, Greece.

The Plague of Justinian (named after the Byzantine emperor of the time) spread through Turkey, the whole of the eastern Mediterranean, and parts of Africa and Europe in 541–542 AD. It was the first of three pandemics caused by bubonic plague. As many as 10,000 people died every day in Constantinople (now Istanbul) in 542 and perhaps 300,000 in the city over the course of a year. Some corpses were piled into towers that were roofed over; others were

Outbreaks of disease brought terror to people who did not understand how these infections were passed on.

put onto boats and set adrift as there was no space to bury them all. Between epidemics, people were infected by a host of other diseases, including smallpox, typhus, cholera, measles, malaria, and polio.

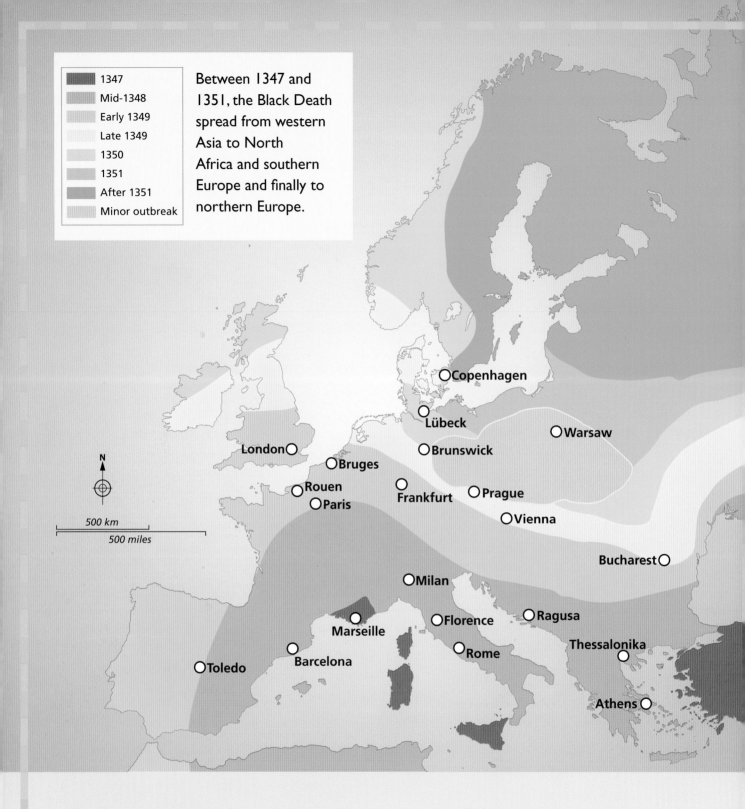

Between 1347 and 1351, the Black Death spread from western Asia to North Africa and southern Europe and finally to northern Europe.

- 1347
- Mid-1348
- Early 1349
- Late 1349
- 1350
- 1351
- After 1351
- Minor outbreak

Copenhagen

Lübeck

Warsaw

Brunswick

London

Bruges

Rouen

Frankfurt

Prague

Paris

Vienna

N

500 km
500 miles

Bucharest

Milan

Florence

Ragusa

Marseille

Rome

Thessalonika

Toledo

Barcelona

Athens

The Black Death

When bubonic plague recurred in Europe in 1346, it was catastrophic. From Mongolia or northern China, the plague spread over a period of a few years to arrive in Europe through Turkey. It killed up to 40 percent of the population of Europe between 1347 and 1351.

Bubonic plague is caused by a parasite that lives in the guts of fleas carried by black rats. When the fleas bite humans, it passes on the disease. Plague can also be transmitted directly between people in droplets breathed or coughed out by sufferers. This causes pneumonic plague and is even more dangerous than the bubonic form. In the Middle Ages, people had no understanding of how diseases were transmitted. Most of their attempts to cure or avoid plague failed.

Recurring Plague

People who caught plague often died a terrible, agonizing death—but not everyone died. Those who survived had immunity. When many people were immune, further epidemics were kept at bay or killed fewer people. Even so, bubonic plague returned intermittently to Europe for several hundred years. Further disastrous epidemics with very high death tolls occurred in parts of Italy in 1576 and 1632. England experienced more outbreaks in 1665–66. In these later outbreaks, some control of the spread was occasionally achieved by using quarantine measures to keep healthy and sick people apart.

Eyam: A Village in Quarantine and a Time Capsule

The English village of Eyam closed all routes in and out after the outbreak of plague in 1665. This prevented the spread of plague to other nearby villages, but at the cost of a high death toll within the village, as even healthy people could not leave.

Now, more than 345 years later, the descendants of plague-survivors in Eyam are of great interest to scientists. Descendants of survivors have a higher incidence of a mutation on a particular gene, Delta 32, than other people. This prevents the plague bacterium from attacking white blood cells. The same mutation appears to give protection against HIV/AIDS, so the study is highly relevant to current medical needs.

PERSPECTIVES

THE BLACK DEATH IN ITALY

Dead bodies filled every corner ... [survivors] carried the bodies out of the houses and laid them at the door; where every morning quantities of the dead might be seen. They then were laid on biers or, as these were often lacking, on tables.

Such was the multitude of corpses ... that there was not enough consecrated ground to give them burial ... they were forced to dig huge trenches, where they buried the bodies by hundreds. Here they stowed them away like bales in the hold of a ship and covered them with a little earth, until the whole trench was full.

Giovanni Boccaccio
Il Decameron Vol. I

Understanding Plague

A later pandemic of bubonic plague finally led scientists to understand how plague is transmitted. Plague broke out in China in 1855 and spread south to Guangzhou, then Hong Kong, and to India by 1896. The French-Swiss doctor and bacteriologist Alexandre Yersin was sent to investigate. Working in a small wooden hut, he identified the bacterium responsible at the same time that a Japanese medical team led by Shibasaburo Kitasato did. The bacterium is now called *Yersinia pestis*.

More Diseases

Although bubonic plague has been responsible for the most dangerous epidemics in history, it is not the only disease to cause chaos and disaster. Indeed, the highest death toll from any single event in history was the result of the 1918 flu pandemic (see pages 24–27).

Smallpox was endemic everywhere except Australia and a few isolated islands for thousands of years. It has killed, paralyzed, or blinded millions of people. Typhus and cholera, highly infectious

FACTS and FIGURES

DEADLY EPIDEMICS IN HISTORY

PLAGUE	DATE (AD)	DISEASE	DEATHS
Plague of Justinian	541–750	Bubonic plague	50–60% of the population of Europe
Black Death	1347–51	Bubonic plague	25–75% of the population of Europe, Asia and Africa
Mexican colonial epidemics	1518–68	Smallpox, typhus, measles	17 million of the indigenous population of 20 million; half the remainder died in the following 50 years
First European flu epidemics	1556–60	Flu	20% of infected people
European smallpox epidemic	18th century	Smallpox	60 million
European tuberculosis epidemic	19th century	Tuberculosis (TB)	25% of the adult population
1918 flu pandemic (Spanish flu)	1918–20	Flu	Between 50 and 100 million

Source: World Health Organization

digestive disorders that cause death through dehydration, thrive in poor, crowded conditions. Diseases spread quickly through the new cities that sprang up in Europe and America during the Industrial Revolution. In the early twentieth century, epidemics of polio raged through cities as cholera was declining. Ironically, the cleaner water supply that saved people from cholera meant that city dwellers were no longer exposed to small doses of polio from birth and did not develop immunity. Instead, the disease hit them full force in the annual summer epidemics. Polio, which can cause paralysis or death, left thousands of people living in artificial respirators called iron lungs. The development of a vaccine in 1952 halted the spread of the disease.

Infection Changes History

Infectious diseases can change the course of history. The plague of Athens may have contributed to the fall of the great ancient Greek civilization. The Plague of Justinian prevented Justinian from regenerating the Roman Empire. The Black Death killed so many people in Europe that farms lay deserted, and famine followed the plague. The shortage of farm workers meant that the survivors could demand better conditions. Some historians suggest the plague helped to end the feudal system.

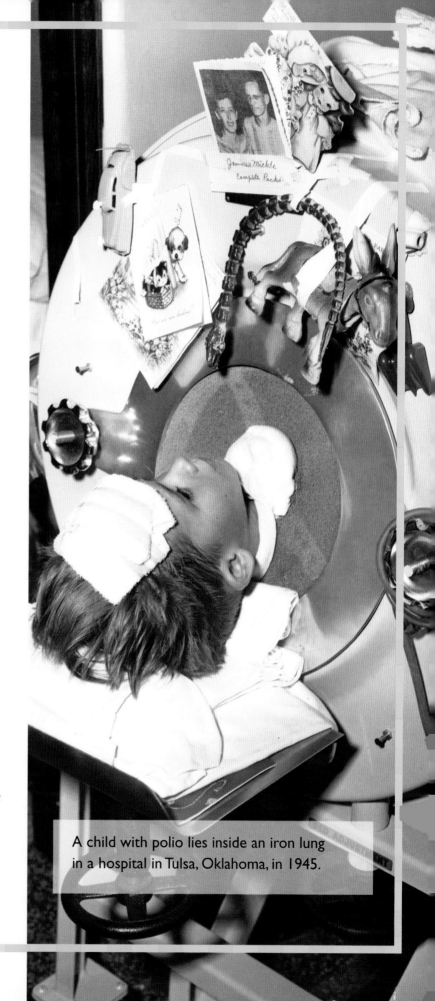

A child with polio lies inside an iron lung in a hospital in Tulsa, Oklahoma, in 1945.

The Threat of Disease Today

Epidemics and pandemics present a sudden and extreme challenge to the world's health and medical institutions, but endemic disease is a constant problem. There are many dangerous infectious diseases that cause death or severe illness on a daily basis.

Killer Mosquitoes

Every year, as many as 2 million people die of malaria, an infectious disease endemic in many tropical and subtropical countries.

Malaria is caused by a parasite carried by the Anopheles mosquito. When the mosquito feeds on an infected person, blood containing malaria parasites is

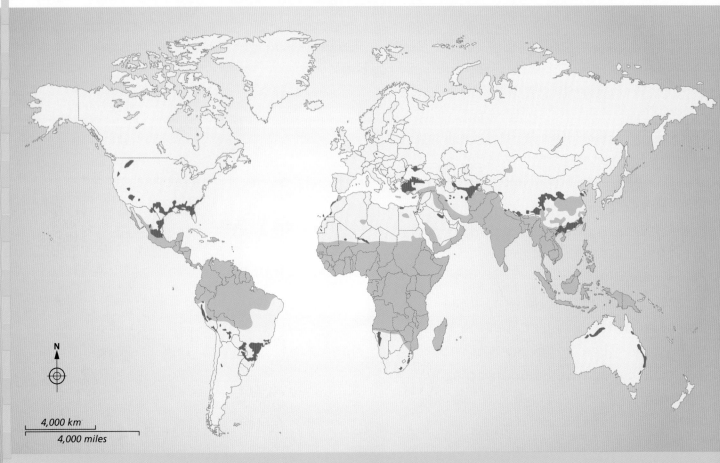

4,000 km

4,000 miles

Areas affected by malaria in 2000

Possible extended range of malaria by 2050 due to global warming

This map shows the parts of the world currently prone to malaria and its likely spread due to climate change.

carried to the mosquito's intestines, where the parasite grows. After about a week, the parasite moves to the salivary glands of the mosquito. When the mosquito next bites someone, parasites mixed with saliva are injected into the person's blood. The parasites travel to the liver. After a period varying from a week to several years, the parasites leave the liver to live and multiply in the red blood cells. As the parasites mature, they burst and infect other blood cells. When this happens, toxins flood the blood, causing malaria's flu-like symptoms of fever, chills, aches, and pains. If untreated, this may lead to loss of red and white blood cells, severe organ damage, reduced blood flow to the brain, and death.

Mosquitoes breed in stagnant water, so malaria is common in hot, swampy areas. As climate change progresses, the areas affected by malaria will spread. The disease is expected to return to parts of Italy as the average summer temperature rises. It had been wiped out in 1970 after a long campaign involving spraying with the insecticide DDT.

Fleas, Ticks, and Other Disease Vectors

Many other bugs are involved in transmitting diseases. Bubonic plague is harbored by fleas that live on rabbits, bobcats, and even domestic cats in the United States and on desert rodents in Mongolia and China. Lyme disease is carried by ticks that live on deer and mice and is a growing problem in the United States. Chagas' disease is carried by the blood-sucking assassin bug, which can live on opossums, raccoons, armadillos, squirrels, wood rats, and mice. It is most common in Central and South America, where it affects 8 million to 10 million people and kills approximately 20,000 people a year. Sleeping sickness (African trypanosomiasis) is carried by the tsetse fly. It is endemic in parts of Africa where it kills more than 40,000 people a year. An epidemic of sleeping sickness in Uganda in 1901 killed more than 250,000 people—two-thirds of the population of the affected area.

CASE STUDY

PLAGUE IN TIBET

In 1966, a hunter in Tibet killed a large rodent, skinned it, and took the pelt to his tented settlement. He fell ill, then his family fell ill, followed by everyone who lived nearby. When investigators came from the capital, they found that the hunter and 13 of his family and neighbors had died of plague—caught from fleas on the rodent he had killed.

The Latest Pandemic

Pandemics are not a thing of the past. The world is currently in the grip of an HIV/AIDS pandemic. AIDS is caused by the human immunodeficiency virus (HIV). Identified in 1981, it is a fairly new disease that emerged in Africa in the late nineteenth or early twentieth century. HIV prevents the human body from defending itself against disease, and AIDS causes death when the body is overwhelmed by infections.

How HIV/AIDS Spreads

HIV/AIDS spreads through direct contact with infected body fluids, such as blood or semen. It may be passed on by sexual contact, during birth, breastfeeding, using infected hypodermic needles, and by blood transfusions with infected blood. In the 1980s, some patients who received medicines made from donated blood contracted HIV/AIDS before its presence in blood was detected.

There is no risk from blood transfusions in most developed countries as all blood is now tested before use. But blood transfusions in China are a source of infection to both recipients of infected blood and blood donors because of the particular techniques China uses to collect blood from donors.

A Slow Pandemic

Because it can take many years for symptoms to emerge, HIV/AIDS is easily passed on to others by people who are unaware they are infected. HIV/AIDS was already well established in Africa and had been carried to other countries before it was identified. It spread quickly through the homosexual community and intravenous drug users in the early 1980s, particularly in the United States, and spread around the world in the course of 10 to 20 years. The most common means of transmission in the United States is male to male sexual contact.

FACTS and FIGURES

HIV/AIDS INFECTION

At the end of 2008, 33.4 million people around the world were living with HIV/AIDS—2.1 million were children.

In 2008, 2.7 million people became infected with HIV/AIDS and 2 million died, including 280,000 children.

Two-thirds of all people infected with HIV/AIDS live in sub-Saharan Africa, including 1.8 million children.

Of the 16 million intravenous drug users in the world, 3 million have HIV.

Worldwide, 10% of new HIV cases are intravenous drug users, but in Russia and eastern Europe, 80% of new cases are drug users.

Source: World Health Organization

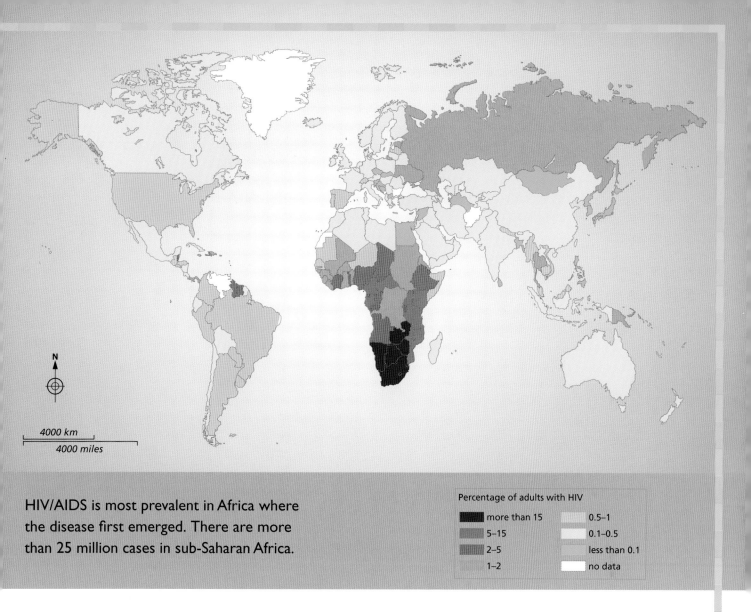

HIV/AIDS is most prevalent in Africa where the disease first emerged. There are more than 25 million cases in sub-Saharan Africa.

Percentage of adults with HIV

more than 15	0.5–1
5–15	0.1–0.5
2–5	less than 0.1
1–2	no data

Treating HIV/AIDS

Antiretroviral (ARV) drugs are available and slow the progress of HIV/AIDS. However, there is no outright cure, and ARVs are too expensive for most people. Patients in developed countries are more likely to receive ARVs. In sub-Saharan Africa and other poor regions, fewer than half of those with HIV/AIDS receive the drugs. With ARV treatment, an HIV-positive person can live for 20 years after infection—twice as long as an untreated person may live.

In the absence of a cure for HIV/AIDS from conventional medicine, some patients have sought treatment from alternative therapies, including Chinese medicine, acupuncture, and homeopathy. Some people put their lives at risk by rejecting ARVs in favor of therapies with no proven benefit. Because those with HIV/AIDS eventually die from secondary infections, improved nutrition and a healthy lifestyle can help prolong their lives.

The funeral procession of a victim of Ebola fever in Kikwit, Zaire. The 1995 epidemic killed 245 people.

Old Diseases Pass Away

Some diseases that have wrought havoc in the past are rarely encountered today. Smallpox causes fever, extreme pain, and a disfiguring rash that covers the entire body. It can lead to paralysis, blindness, mental disability, and death. It is the largest single cause of death in history, killing 300 million people in the twentieth century. Due to successful vaccination campaigns, smallpox was completely eradicated in nature by 1979 (but samples have been kept for research in the United States and Russia).

Some diseases described in ancient times cannot be identified and may have died out naturally. Leprosy (Hanson's disease) was common in medieval Europe, but it declined naturally for no known reason. Other diseases have been greatly reduced by vaccination campaigns and improved hygiene and living conditions. Diseases that caused many deaths in the nineteenth and twentieth centuries, including cholera, tuberculosis, polio, diphtheria, whooping cough, and typhus, are now uncommon in most developed countries, but they can still afflict less developed areas.

New Diseases

While some old diseases disappear, new ones emerge. Fortunately, some of the most frightening new diseases are quite rare. Ebola, Lassa, and dengue fevers are deadly hemorrhagic fevers. Ebola fever, the most deadly, emerged in Sudan in 1976. It causes flu-like symptoms and bleeding from bodily orifices as internal organs begin to dissolve. Ebola is fatal in 50 to 90 percent of cases, depending on the strain. People become so ill with Ebola fever that it rarely spreads outside a small area, as sufferers are too sick to travel. Even so, the virus is highly contagious, and people caring for sufferers often fall ill with the disease unless they use rigorous barrier nursing methods. New forms of flu and other respiratory diseases threaten more widespread infection, but with a lower mortality rate (see pages 26–29).

CASE STUDY

EBOLA FEVER

Rose Akello, 38, fell ill with fever and bleeding in her hut in Gulu, Uganda. Her family nursed her until she died, then washed her body for burial. Within a week, her two-week-old baby, 13-year-old daughter, and husband fell victim to the disease and died. When Ebola was identified, the town panicked, but dozens of other people had already been infected.

Mutation

The microorganisms that cause disease change very rapidly through a process called mutation. The mutation rate of viruses is higher than that of bacteria, so viruses adapt more quickly to new environments and threats to their survival. When a virus or bacterium changes, natural or acquired immunity does not always protect people from the new strain. For this reason, a new disease can spread very rapidly through a community or across the world.

Pandemic!

Pandemics have recurred throughout history, and there is no reason to assume they will not continue. The most likely type of disease to produce a pandemic in the modern world is a viral respiratory disease such as flu. With air travel and a highly mobile world population, a pandemic disease would spread more quickly now than ever before.

Flu in the Past

The first European flu epidemic occurred in 1556–60 and killed 20 percent of infected people. There have been flu epidemics ever since. The most deadly flu pandemic started in 1918, just after World War I. A particularly virulent strain of flu, often called Spanish flu, swept around the world in several waves. Between the first and second waves, the virus changed and became much more deadly. Spanish flu killed more people than World War I and reached every part of the world. The mortality rate varied widely, from 0.4 percent to 30 percent among different populations and killed between 50 and 100 million people.

Flu usually affects children, the very old, and those who are already weakened in some way. But Spanish flu was most deadly among young, healthy adults with a strong immune system. It produced an extreme response, causing the immune system to go into overdrive and destroy the body's own tissues in its attempt to defeat the virus. People died from suffocation as blood flooded their lungs.

PERSPECTIVES

DEATH ON THE WARDS IN 1918

The morgues were packed almost to the ceiling with bodies stacked one on top of another. The morticians worked day and night. You could never turn around without seeing a big, red truck loaded with caskets for the train station so bodies could be sent home.

We didn't have the time to treat [patients]. We didn't take temperatures; we didn't even have time to take blood pressure. We would give them a little hot whisky toddy; that's about all we had time to do.

Josie Brown, nurse at the Naval Hospital in Great Lakes, Illinois, in 1918

Volunteers wearing masks fed the children of flu-stricken families during the 1918 pandemic.

H1N1 Flu, Bird Flu, and People

The flu virus can change and grow in animal reservoirs—often pigs and birds—before infecting people with a new strain. The deadly 1918 flu, a variety known as H1N1, came from pigs. The avian (bird) flu that appeared in the Far East in the 1990s was an H5N1 variety that passes from birds directly to people. A new strain of flu that passed from animals to humans can cause an epidemic only if it changes so that it can be transmitted directly between people. A strain that must always pass from an animal to a human does not present a pandemic threat.

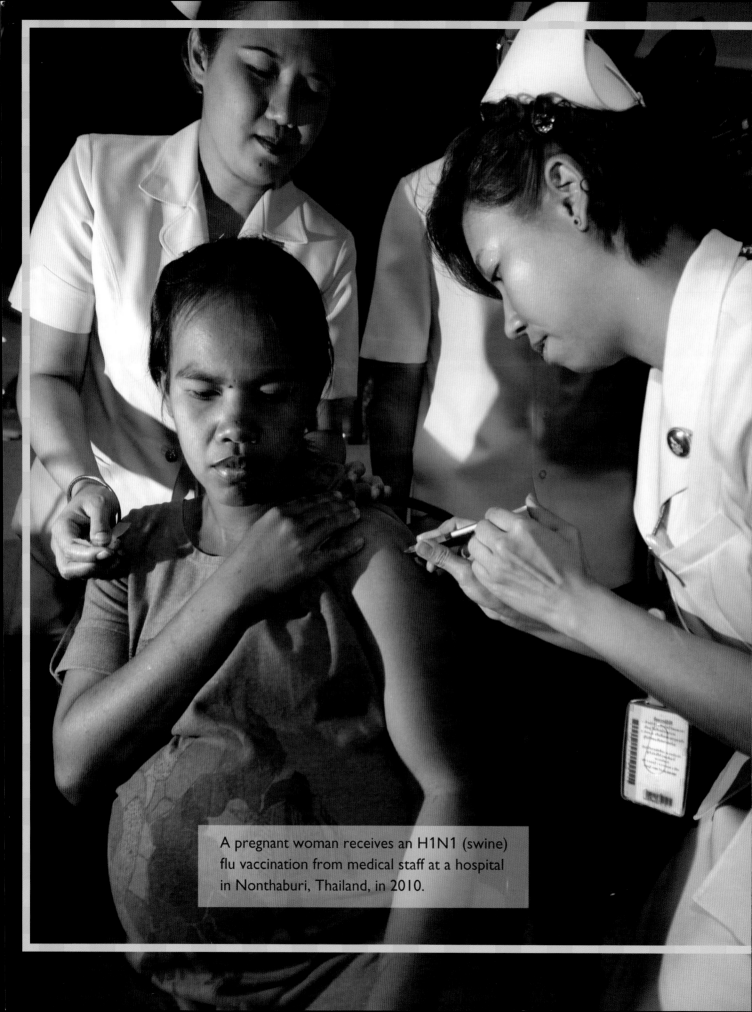

A pregnant woman receives an H1N1 (swine) flu vaccination from medical staff at a hospital in Nonthaburi, Thailand, in 2010.

Studying 1918 Flu

Scientists study the pandemic diseases of the past in an attempt to understand what they were, how they spread, and whether they are related to present diseases. Because the 1918 flu was so deadly, it has been the focus of study in recent years. Flu is caused by a virus, which is little more than a strand of DNA (a chemical carrying genetic information). The genome (the complete set of genes in an organism) of the 1918 flu has been studied from samples of the virus that were recovered from bodies preserved in the frozen tundra of northern Canada. Scientists have regenerated the virus in order to study it in more detail. Research such as this can help us to understand how a virus works and develop treatments and vaccines. Understanding the 1918 flu virus will make it easier to identify a similarly dangerous strain if it emerges in the future and help us to fight it.

Flu and Immunity

People are frequently exposed to flu viruses, and many have developed immunity to some strains of flu. When a new strain emerges, it can cause a pandemic because no one has immunity. Afterward, the population may have immunity that lasts many decades, and a related strain is unlikely to cause a new pandemic soon.

Even seasonal flu can be dangerous. People considered at risk, such as the elderly, are offered vaccinations against it. The flu virus regularly mutates, and the seasonal flu vaccine has to be reengineered each year to suit the newest form. Any new pandemic flu would need a new vaccine. This takes many months to develop, so a pandemic strain will take hold before we can guard against it. Slowing the spread of a new form of flu, using measures such as quarantine and closing international borders, gives medical scientists the best chance of developing a vaccine to reduce the total number of infections and deaths.

There were dangerous epidemics of Asian flu in 1956–57 (1 million to 1.5 million dead) and Hong Kong flu in 1968–69 (0.75 million to 1 million dead). In 1976, a threatened pandemic of swine flu led to a mass vaccination program in the United States. The pandemic did not take hold, but some people who received the vaccine fell ill and died.

CASE STUDY

THE 1976 SWINE FLU DEBACLE

Scientists feared that an outbreak of swine flu in 1976 would become a pandemic affecting 50 to 60 million Americans. Forty million Americans (25 percent of the population) were vaccinated against swine flu. But there were only approximately 200 cases of swine flu in the United States and one death. However, 25 died and more than 500 people developed Guillain-Barré syndrome after receiving the vaccine.

SARS, Avian Flu, and H1N1

The world may have had a near miss in 2002 when a new and deadly respiratory disease called SARS (severe acute respiratory syndrome) emerged in China. It caused breathing difficulties and killed approximately 10 percent of sufferers. Carried by international air travel, SARS spread rapidly from China to 37 countries worldwide. More than 8,000 people were infected and 774 died. Strict quarantine of sufferers and contacts helped contain the virus and avoided a pandemic.

A very dangerous form of avian flu, which first appeared in China in 1987, kills approximately 60 percent of people who catch it. Currently, the virus does not pass readily between people—almost all human cases have been caught directly from birds. It will only become a widespread threat if it mutates so that it can pass directly between people. If that occurs, it may also become less dangerous, but it could still be more deadly than other forms of flu.

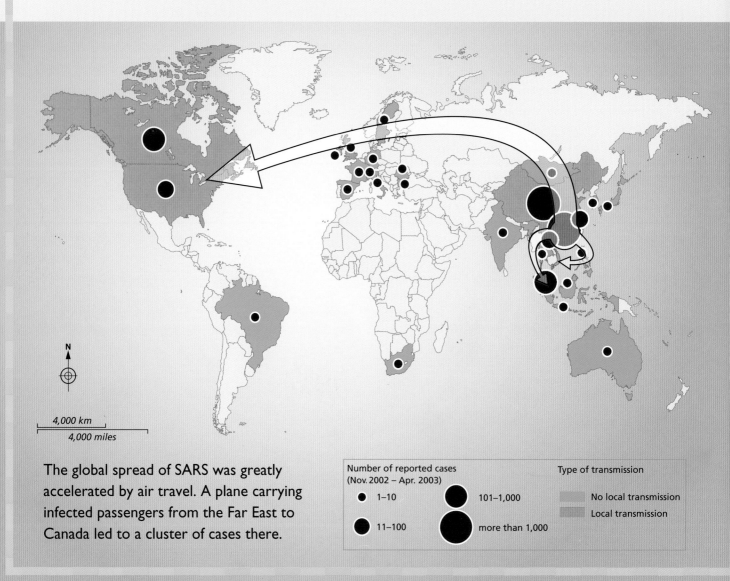

4,000 km

4,000 miles

The global spread of SARS was greatly accelerated by air travel. A plane carrying infected passengers from the Far East to Canada led to a cluster of cases there.

Number of reported cases
(Nov. 2002 – Apr. 2003)

- 1–10
- 11–100
- 101–1,000
- more than 1,000

Type of transmission

No local transmission
Local transmission

FACTS and FIGURES

WHO (WORLD HEALTH ORGANIZATION) PANDEMIC FLU ALERT LEVELS

The WHO operates a scale of pandemic alert levels as follows:

1 Flu in animals has not affected humans.

2 A strain of flu circulating in animals has affected humans.

3 Flu caught from animals never or rarely transmits between people.

4 Flu transmits between people enough to infect a community.

5 Flu transmission between people has spread between countries.

6 Pandemic is happening.

Source: World Health Organization

An H1N1 flu pandemic that began in Mexico in April 2009 provoked a major scare. By mid-2010 it had caused more than 18,000 deaths worldwide.

Pandemic Planning

The World Health Organization (WHO) monitors newly emerging flu strains and patterns of transmission. Governments and health care organizations use computer modeling software to predict how a pandemic might spread, the resulting health care requirements, and the economic effects it would have. These computer models are highly sophisticated and can deal with many different scenarios. Computer models are a vital tool in enabling national and international organizations to prepare and plan. Slowing the spread of a disease might buy time to develop a vaccine, but it is unlikely to avert a pandemic entirely.

During a pandemic, essential services, such as electricity and water supplies, may not be available. Food supplies may be restricted, and health care services may be overwhelmed by demand and the lack of staff.

The Fastest Pandemic Ever

The speed with which SARS and the 2009 H1N1 flu spread around the world shows how modern air travel can accelerate the spread of disease. Passengers with no signs of illness when they board a long flight may pass on an illness before the plane lands. Authorities would struggle to suspend air traffic quickly enough to contain a disease in a single country. Pandemic modeling software suggests a flu strain that emerged in the Far East could spread around the world in about a month.

Tackling Disease—Prevention and Cure

Infectious diseases will always be with us. We need to tackle them by preventing the emergence and spread of diseases and by treating people who become ill. This is not just a matter for medical science. Politics, economics, education, town planning, and social engineering also play parts in the fight against infectious disease.

Public Health

Many diseases are spread by dirty water that is contaminated by human waste. A clean water supply is one of the most important requirements for a healthy population. In the nineteenth century, six cholera pandemics caused millions of deaths in Europe, Africa, and the Americas. The installation of sewers put an end to cholera outbreaks in the cities of the developed world. However, infections from drinking water polluted with sewage continue to kill between 2.5 million and 5 million people a year, mostly in less developed countries. This situation is worsened by wars and natural disasters. Refugees from these events are often forced to live in crowded, unsanitary conditions where the lack of a clean water supply can cause outbreaks of disease.

Food Hygiene

Just as clean water is essential, so is clean food. Food can be contaminated if it is washed and prepared using dirty water or if it is left exposed to air where bacteria or germ-carrying insects can land on it. Disease also can be spread if food is prepared or served by people with dirty hands or by people who have infectious disease. In a famous historical case in the

CASE STUDY

KAKUMA REFUGEE CAMP, KENYA

Kakuma camp opened in 1992. It is home to approximately 50,000 people forced from their homes by war or persecution. It is run by the United Nations. Cholera periodically sweeps through the camp, killing hundreds. Unfortunately, breweries and food outlets have helped the spread of disease by using unclean water. The camp is often infested with flies and lacks proper toilet facilities.

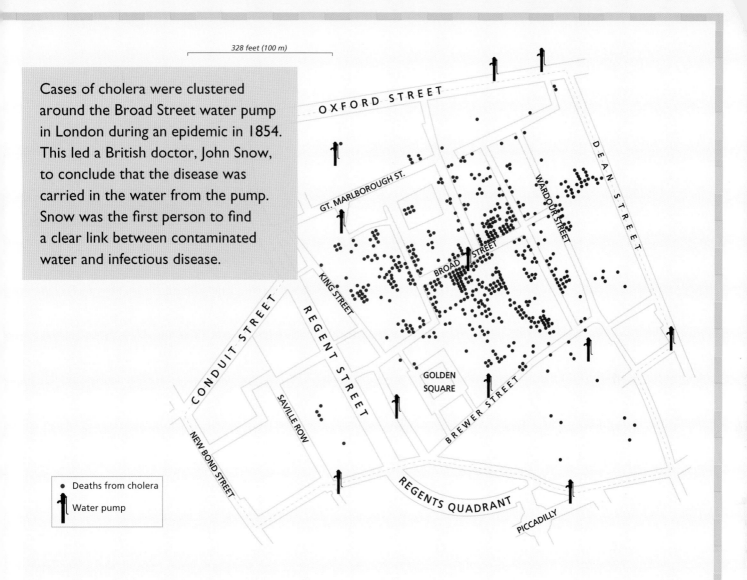

Cases of cholera were clustered around the Broad Street water pump in London during an epidemic in 1854. This led a British doctor, John Snow, to conclude that the disease was carried in the water from the pump. Snow was the first person to find a clear link between contaminated water and infectious disease.

• Deaths from cholera

Water pump

United States, Mary Mallon, nicknamed Typhoid Mary, infected 53 people with typhoid while working as a cook. A carrier of the disease, she never suffered from it herself. Colds, flu, and gastric disorders are easily passed on by infected people preparing food or by poor food hygiene.

Death to Insects

Killing or avoiding insects is the best way to combat insect-borne diseases. For individuals, wearing thick clothing and using mosquito nets and insect repellent can help. But to protect entire communities, authorities must kill the insects or destroy their habitats. Getting rid of stagnant water helps destroy colonies of mosquitoes that carry malaria, dengue fever, and other diseases. Insecticide spray kills insects of many types, but it also destroys harmless insects and disrupts the ecosystem. In some places, biological solutions have succeeded. This includes introducing predators such as bats to eat insects.

Vaccination

Vaccination works by giving people a small dose of a disease-causing bacterium or virus to make their immune systems produce antibodies to combat the disease. Many vaccines contain either weakened or dead bacteria or viruses. In a live or attenuated vaccine, the microorganisms that cause disease have been changed so that they have lost their virulence but still will prompt the body to make antibodies. Sometimes, an attenuated vaccine uses a related, but less dangerous, disease that prompts wide enough immunity to cover the dangerous disease as well. In a dead vaccine, the microorganisms have been killed by heat or chemicals. Generally, live vaccines provide better protection in healthy adults, but dead vaccines are safer for people who may be at risk from even a mild form of the live disease.

Understanding Germs and Vaccines

The first safe vaccination was developed in 1796 by an English country doctor, Edward Jenner, who noticed that milkmaids with sores from cowpox never contracted smallpox. He used pus from cowpox sores to inoculate people against smallpox.

Jenner's smallpox vaccine worked, but he did not know why. No one understood how germs caused infections. In the mid-nineteenth century, Louis Pasteur showed that diseases could be passed on by

microscopic particles—later identified as bacteria and viruses.

During the twentieth century, vaccination against deadly diseases, such as diphtheria and polio, reduced childhood deaths and suffering. Parents once lived in terror of their children contracting a serious infectious disease during one of the many epidemics, but death from infectious disease is now rare in developed countries. It is a challenge for the WHO to bring the benefits of vaccination to children living in less developed countries, particularly those in remote areas. Vaccines need to be kept clean and cold and given using sterile needles, which presents practical problems in many areas of the world.

Preparation and Panic

Sometimes, vaccination scares or errors lead the public to reject protection. In 1955, approximately 120,000 children in the United States received a dangerous live polio vaccine—and many developed polio. The 1976 swine flu vaccine (see page 27) killed more Americans than the disease it was supposed to protect them from. In 1998, a medical paper claimed there was a link between the MMR (measles, mumps, and rubella) vaccine and autism. Many parents in the United States and the United Kingdom refused the vaccine. An increase in dangerous cases of measles followed.

When vaccination programs are successful, the incidence of disease falls. Eventually, negative reactions to the vaccine may become a greater risk than the disease itself. Immunization is then given only to people at a greater than average risk of catching the disease.

When Edward Jenner introduced a vaccine for smallpox, he and his vaccine were ridiculed, as depicted in this cartoon by James Gilray.

The Cow-Pock — or — the Wonderful Effects of the New Inoculation ! — Vide the Publications of ye Anti-Vaccine Society.

Women and children in Orissa, India, listen to an instructor teaching them about precautions against malaria.

Education

One of the most effective ways of preventing the spread of infectious disease is by educating people in safe practices. Hand washing is the single most effective protection against food contamination and airborne diseases such as flu. Other protective measures that can be spread through public health education include vaccination, observing food hygiene procedures, using mosquito nets to protect against malaria, and practicing safe sex (using a condom) to protect against sexually transmitted infections such as HIV/AIDS. Drug addicts can be taught to protect themselves against HIV/AIDS by never reusing hypodermic needles. Education is the main means of combating the spread of HIV/AIDs, but this has been hampered by religious and social objections to discussing sex, promoting contraceptive use, and operating needle exchange programs.

Educating Travelers

Travelers are often exposed to new diseases that are not endemic in their homelands. To protect travelers from infection and to prevent them from introducing a disease to their community on their return home, they are usually vaccinated against infections common in the places they are visiting. In the case of malaria, for which there is no vaccine, a course of tablets protects against infection. Visitors also need to be instructed about taking suitable precautions to avoid disease. This includes not drinking water that may be unsafe, protecting themselves against insect bites, and avoiding exposure to water-borne parasites.

Treatment and Cure

It is better, cheaper, and easier to prevent the spread of disease than to treat people who have become infected. But when prevention fails, treatment is necessary. In developed countries, most people have access to a high level of health care and can expect professional nursing and treatment with antibiotics and antiviral medicines. In less developed countries, and in times of pandemic, war, and natural disaster, this level of care is not always available.

Developing new vaccines and effective treatments for disease involves long-term, expensive scientific research and extensive testing. As the boundaries of medical science advance, and more complex and sophisticated forms of treatment are developed, more lives can be saved. But the organizations developing them need to recoup their costs. This means many treatments are available only to individuals and communities that can pay a high price for them.

The Future of Infectious Diseases

Diseases change as bacteria and viruses mutate. But it is not only time that causes them to evolve. Changes in the way we live alter the types of threat presented by disease and sometimes bring about changes in infections.

Bacteria Fight Back

The development of antibiotics was a breakthrough. Within a few years in the early twentieth century, many previously untreatable and often deadly infections could be cured. Yet in a frighteningly short time, some diseases have become resistant to the antibiotics that were once effective against them, and these altered diseases are very difficult to treat.

Infections become resistant to antibiotics when the antibiotics are overused or misused. When bacteria are exposed to low doses of a drug, some develop a chemical composition that the drug can no longer combat.

The widespread use of antibiotics in farm animals has led to small quantities remaining in the food chain and entering the water supply. These tiny doses of antibiotics have enabled bacteria to develop resistance to the drugs. When individuals are prescribed antibiotics and do not finish taking them, perhaps because they feel well again, any bacteria remaining in their bodies can develop into a resistant strain. These may infect other people or cause the same person to fall ill again, but this time with a form of the disease that is more difficult to treat.

Back to Basics

In the nineteenth century, Florence Nightingale and Ignaz Semmelweis made progress against infection by insisting on

PERSPECTIVES

EPIDEMIC OF MRSA

Reports [of rising rates of MRSA] highlight our concern over the crisis of antibiotic resistance, a problem that is magnified because there simply aren't enough new drugs in the pharmaceutical pipeline to keep pace with the evolution of drug-resistant bacteria, the so-called "superbugs." This crisis has the potential to touch us all because drug-resistant infections can strike anyone—young or old, healthy or chronically ill.

Joseph R. Dalovisio, MD, President of the Infectious Diseases Society of America

A highly magnified image of the staphylococcus bacterium responsible for MRSA.

cleanliness in hospitals. Nightingale cleaned up the hospital wards at Scutari, Turkey, during the Crimean War. Semmelweis insisted doctors in the hospital in Vienna wash their hands before delivering babies. Hand washing and hygiene remain major weapons in the battle against infection.

Today, the antibiotic-resistant superbugs *Clostridium difficile* and MRSA (methicillin-resistant *Staphylococcus aureus*) are a major cause of illness and death in many hospitals in developed countries. MRSA can cause necrotizing fasciitis (the "flesh-eating bug"). This is an infection that eats away skin and muscle, causing pain, deformity, and sometimes death. Superbugs can only be treated with a complex combination of drugs, and treatment is not always successful. The best way of combating superbugs is the deep cleaning of hospitals to try to eradicate every trace of the bacteria responsible.

The Bioterrorist Threat

Not all infection is accidental—sometimes diseases are used as weapons. In 1346, a Mongol army catapulted the corpses of plague victims over the walls of the besieged city of Kaffa to spread infection there. In World War II, the Japanese army used jars of plague-infected fleas against the Chinese. Today, government security services are concerned about bioterrorism—terrorists using infectious diseases as weapons. Many diseases, including anthrax, plague, and smallpox, could easily be weaponized. These infections could quickly spread through a population and overwhelm medical services. In addition, these diseases would be hard to contain. An attack on one city may quickly develop into a pandemic that ravages continents or the entire world. Religious fundamentalist terrorists sometimes do not worry about this threat, trusting that true believers would be saved.

Anthrax Through the Mail

In 2001, several news outlets in the United States and two U.S. senators received packages in the mail that contained a white powder. The powder contained anthrax spores. Five people died as a result of infection with anthrax, and 68 others were harmed. The packages were sent by Bruce Edwards Ivins, a scientist working in the U.S. government's biodefense laboratories. He committed suicide before he was caught.

Planning for Catastrophe

National and international health care organizations try to predict the spread of infectious disease and make plans for coping with epidemics and pandemics. Computer models show how different diseases, starting in different places, may spread and the impact they will have on health care services, the economy, and the infrastructure of communities.

The lessons of past pandemics show that social disruption may cause as many problems as the disease. The supply of food, water, electricity, and other essential services may be disrupted by staff sickness.

CASE STUDY

PANDEMIC RESPONSE: 2009 FLU IN THE UNITED KINGDOM

The H1N1 flu outbreak, which began in 2009, affected many countries of the world. In the United Kingdom, measures to restrict the spread of the disease included:

- closing schools when the virus was identified in pupils;
- urging people to choose a flu buddy—someone who could collect medicines and buy food for them if they fell ill, so they did not need to go out and expose others to the virus;
- providing Tamiflu (a treatment for flu) to infected people in the early stages of the epidemic to reduce symptoms and cut infection rates.

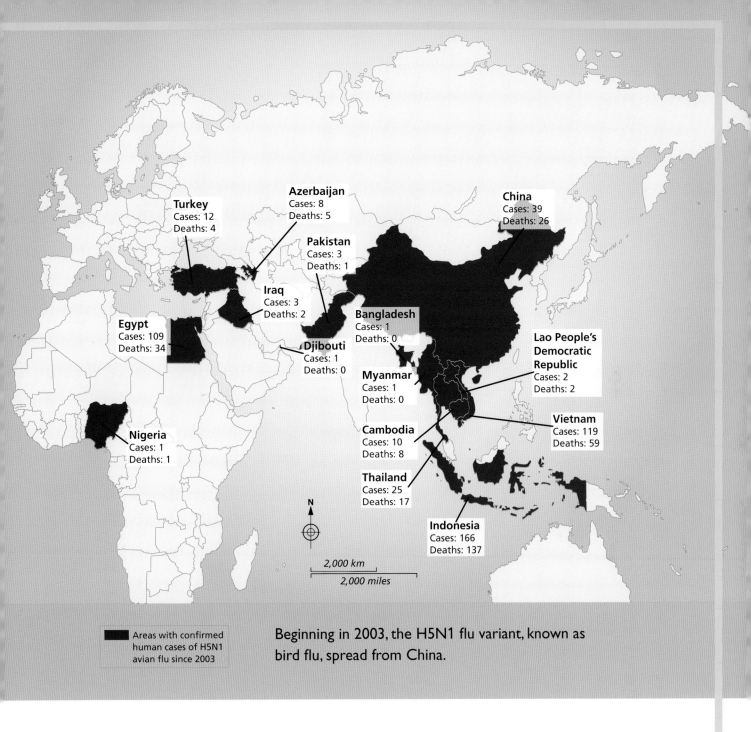

Turkey
Cases: 12
Deaths: 4

Azerbaijan
Cases: 8
Deaths: 5

China
Cases: 39
Deaths: 26

Pakistan
Cases: 3
Deaths: 1

Iraq
Cases: 3
Deaths: 2

Egypt
Cases: 109
Deaths: 34

Bangladesh
Cases: 1
Deaths: 0

Lao People's Democratic Republic
Cases: 2
Deaths: 2

Djibouti
Cases: 1
Deaths: 0

Myanmar
Cases: 1
Deaths: 0

Nigeria
Cases: 1
Deaths: 1

Vietnam
Cases: 119
Deaths: 59

Cambodia
Cases: 10
Deaths: 8

Thailand
Cases: 25
Deaths: 17

Indonesia
Cases: 166
Deaths: 137

N

2,000 km
2,000 miles

Areas with confirmed human cases of H5N1 avian flu since 2003

Beginning in 2003, the H5N1 flu variant, known as bird flu, spread from China.

At the height of the flu pandemic of 1918, bodies were piled in the streets. Children orphaned by flu sometimes starved in their houses. Pandemic planning aims to avoid such terrible consequences by predicting requirements and providing the necessary resources.

Governments may consider slowing the spread of a pandemic by closing international borders, suspending air travel, and imposing quarantine or travel restrictions on people.

Continuing the Fight Against Disease

The fight against disease is unlikely to end. As science advances, we discover new ways of tackling disease, but also uncover new threats. Climate change brings additional challenges as some tropical and subtropical diseases are taking hold in new areas.

The Search for Treatments

Many antibiotics and other drug-based treatments for infectious diseases occur naturally in plants and fungi. The search for these is often a matter of trial and error. Scientists first look at species related to those that have already provided useful drugs or investigate plants used in traditional medicine. Approximately two-thirds of all plant species live in tropical rainforests, and relatively few have been studied by medical science. There still may be a lot to be discovered in nature's medicine chest.

Pushing the Boundaries

Not all medicines come from the natural world. Some modern medicines are designed using computers combined with a knowledge of the chemical actions of disease-causing bacteria and viruses. For example, to make an antiviral drug to combat a flu virus, scientists might examine the molecular structure of the virus's protein coat. They can then design a molecule that will lock into key sites on the virus and prevent it from reproducing inside the cells of the body. The next challenge is to make a molecule with the right structure and deliver it in such a way that it will target and disable the virus.

PERSPECTIVES

RISKY RESEARCH

Once the genetic sequence [of the 1918 flu virus] is publicly available, there's a theoretical risk that any molecular biologist with sufficient knowledge could recreate this virus.

Dr. John Wood, virologist,
National Institute for Biological
Standards and Control, United Kingdom

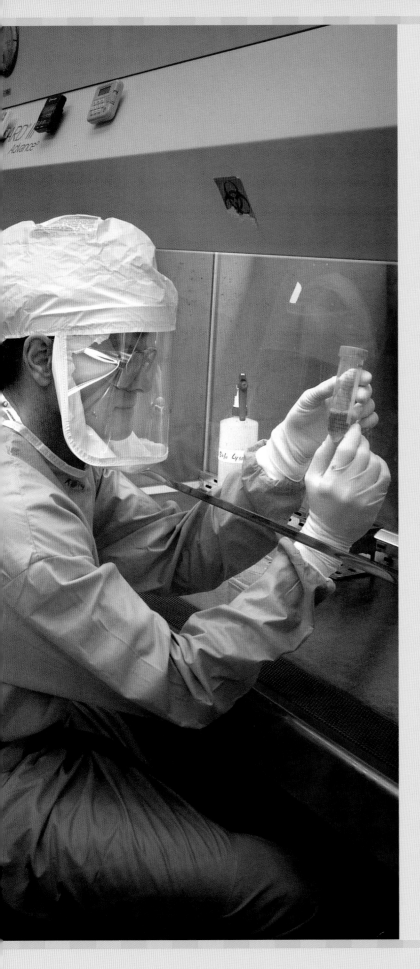

Working with Genomes

Every living organism has a genome, which is a set of chromosomes (long molecules of DNA) that contain the DNA for that organism. The order in which certain chemical blocks, called bases, appear in a DNA molecule acts as a code defining the characteristics of the organism. When scientists sequence a genome, they work out the order of these bases. A virus is little more than a strand of DNA with a protein coat—it may not even count as a living organism. Understanding the genome of a virus makes it easier for medical scientists to find ways to interact with the virus and prevent its action. Scientists have re-created the 1918 flu virus in the hope of better understanding why it had such devastating effects.

Sequencing its genome also makes it possible to create a virus. The possibility that scientists or terrorists could genetically engineer a completely new virus, against which we have no defense, is no longer just science fiction.

Dr. Terrence Tumpey, who re-created the 1918 flu virus, works with a sample of the virus in a special biosafety laboratory at the Centers for Disease Control and Prevention (CDC) in the United States.

New Ways to Fight Disease

The difficulty of keeping vaccines safe while delivering them to remote regions may be resolved in some imaginative ways. Using genetic engineering techniques, it is now possible to integrate some vaccines into foods. One pilot project has produced a variety of banana that provides immunity to polio. It is easier to deliver a banana to a child in a remote Indian village than a vaccine, which must be kept cool and injected with a sterile needle by trained staff. The child only has to eat the banana to gain protection against polio.

Genetic engineering may help combat disease in other ways too. Scientists have tried to bioengineer mosquitoes incapable of hosting the malaria parasite and releasing them where they may take over the Anopheles mosquito. So far, though, scientists have not managed to produce mosquitoes that are able to compete and survive.

Eaten from Within

Antibiotic-resistant bacteria may be combated with bacteriophages. These viruses attack and destroy bacteria. Bacteriophages have been used in treatment in the former Soviet Union and Eastern Europe since 1950, but they have not been explored extensively as a treatment elsewhere. Their use is probably much older. In many places, the waters of particular rivers (including the Ganges) were found to have some curative effect on certain diseases—perhaps due to the presence of bacteriophages.

Polio was eradicated in the United States by the vaccination policies of the 1950s but remained endemic in many parts of the world in 1988.

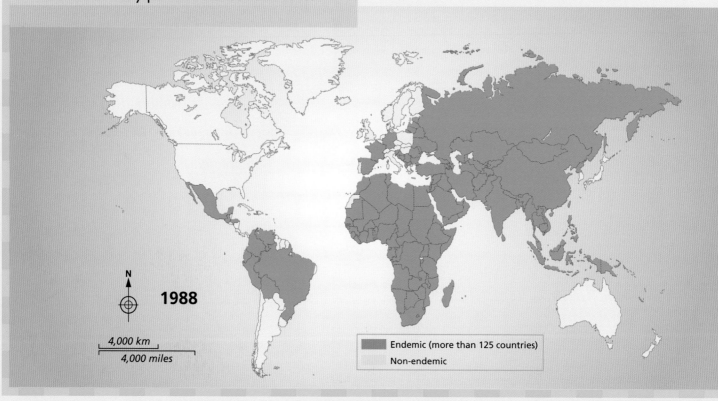

1988

4,000 km
4,000 miles

Endemic (more than 125 countries)
Non-endemic

Out of This World

Exploration has always brought people into contact with new diseases and spread explorers' diseases to new communities. There is little of the world left to discover, but we may still come across new—or very old—diseases. As the ice caps and permafrost melt due to climate change, disease-causing organisms may be released. Deep sea vents hold forms of life—some of them microscopic—that have never been encountered before. Some could cause disease. Space exploration may be a potential source of alien diseases, or it could make Earth diseases more virulent. Astronauts returning to Earth are quarantined in case of unknown dangers.

CASE STUDY

DEADLY BACTERIA IN SPACE

A 2006 study found that salmonella bacteria taken into space and grown in zero-gravity in the space shuttle were many times more deadly when returned to Earth than normal salmonella. The activity of 167 genes in the bacteria changed in weightless conditions. The bacteria were compared with identical bacteria kept on Earth. Both were used to infect mice. The space bacteria killed many more mice than those grown on Earth. This may have implications for long trips in space as astronauts take many bacteria with them in their bodies.

By 2003, polio had been wiped out in many more countries, remaining only in India and parts of Africa. The change was the successful result of a worldwide drive to eradicate the disease by vaccination.

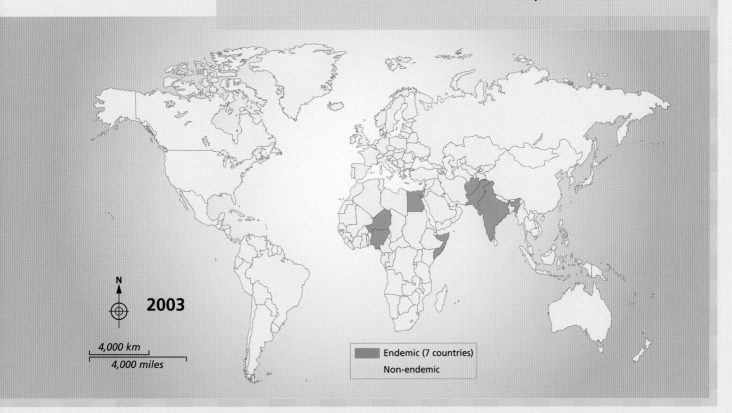

N

2003

4,000 km

4,000 miles

Endemic (7 countries)
Non-endemic

Glossary

AIDS Acquired immune deficiency syndrome: a condition in which the immune system stops working and may eventually lead to death.

anthrax An often fatal bacterial disease that has different symptoms depending on how it is caught.

anthropologist A scientist who studies human society, culture, and development.

antibodies Chemicals produced by white blood cells in response to an infection.

attenuated To reduce the virulence of a virus.

autism Impaired development that results in difficulties relating to others and communicating.

bacterium (plural: bacteria) A type of microorganism that has a cell wall, a nucleus, its own DNA, and is capable of reproducing itself.

bacteriophage A virus that invades and destroys bacteria.

barrier nursing methods Nursing procedures that involve complete protection by using gowns, gloves and masks as well as isolating patients to prevent contamination of medical staff or other patients.

bilharzia A parasitic infection contracted from dirty water that can lead to organ damage.

BSE Bovine spongiform encephalitis: a disease of cattle that causes deterioration of the brain and eventual death.

bubonic plague A bacterial disease that causes fever and painful buboes (boils) and is often fatal.

cholera A gastric disease that causes extreme diarrhea leading to dehydration and often death.

chromosome A strand of DNA that carries genetic information defining the organism.

diphtheria A severe bacterial disease that causes difficulty with breathing and swallowing and may lead to death.

DNA Deoxyribonucleic acid: a complex protein-based chemical that carries genetic information.

dormant Not active, but can become active again.

Ebola fever A disease that causes fever and internal bleeding, usually leading to death.

endemic Occurring naturally in a particular place.

epidemic An outbreak of infectious disease affecting many people.

gene An element of genetic information controlling one aspect of an organism's characteristics.

genetic engineering Working with the genetic composition of an organism to make changes to the organism or produce offspring with particular characteristics.

genome The full sequence of genes in an organism's DNA that defines all its characteristics.

hemorrhagic fevers A group of diseases that causes fever and internal bleeding.

hemophilia A condition in which the blood does not clot and continues to flow if a person is injured.

HIV Human immunodeficiency virus: a virus that causes the immune system to break down.

host An organism in which a microorganism, such as a parasite or bacterium, lives.

immune system The body's defense mechanism.

immunity Protection against disease.

incubation period The time during which a disease is developing but does not yet produce symptoms.

intravenous drug user A person who injects drugs.

leprosy A disease that causes damage to the nerves and leads to deformity, blindness, and deterioration of parts of the body.

malaria A disease carried by parasites in the blood that leads to bouts of fever and may be fatal a long time after infection.

measles A disease that causes fever and a skin rash. It can lead to blindness, brain damage, or death.

microorganism A very small, living organism that can be seen only by using a microscope.

morbidity The relative incidence of disease.

mortality rate The proportion of people infected with a disease who die.

MRSA Methicillin-resistant *Staphylococcus aureus*: an infectious disease that is resistant to antibiotics.

mumps A viral disease that makes the glands swell but does not usually cause lasting damage.

mutation A random change in the genetic composition of an organism.

pandemic A widespread outbreak of a disease.

pneumonic plague A form of plague caused by the same bacterium as bubonic plague but is spread by droplets in the air and affects the lungs. It is a more severe and deadly form of plague than bubonic.

protozoa A single-celled organism.

quarantine Keeping infected or possibly infected people away from others.

reservoir People or animals that host a disease between larger outbreaks.

rubella German measles, an infection that causes fever and a red rash. It is most dangerous to pregnant women.

salmonella A bacterium that causes food poisoning.

sleeping sickness A deadly parasitic disease that damages the nervous system and leads to daytime sleeping and nighttime sleeplessness.

smallpox A viral disease that causes pain, fever, and a disfiguring rash of blisters. It may lead to blindness, paralysis, mental problems, or death.

spore An immature form of an organism.

tuberculosis (TB) An infectious bacterial disease in which nodules called tubercles grow in the tissues, especially the lungs.

typhoid A bacterial disease carried by dirty water. It causes fever and diarrhea.

typhus A parasitic disease that causes mental confusion.

vaccination The use of a small dose of a disease-causing agent to prompt immunity to a disease.

vaccine A substance used to produce immunity to a disease.

virus A type of very simple disease-causing agent that can only reproduce inside a host cell.

whooping cough A cough characterized by a distinctive whooping sound as the sufferer tries to breathe in.

yellow fever A viral disease transmitted by mosquitoes, which gives the skin a yellow tinge. It causes fever, sickness, and pain and can lead to liver damage.

Further Information

Books

Global Aids: Myths and Facts by Alexander Irwin Joyce Millen and Dorothy Fallows (South End Press, 2003)

Pox, Pus and Plague: A History of Disease and Infection by John Townsend (Raintree, 2006)

Germ Killers: Fighting Disease by Sally Morgan (Heinemann, 2009)

Twelve Diseases That Changed Our World by Irwin W. Sherman (American Society for Microbiology (AMS) Press, 2007)

Web Sites

www.healthmap.org/en/
Constantly updating map of disease outbreaks worldwide.

http://medicalcenter.osu.edu/patientcare/healthcare_services/infectious_diseases/immunesystem/Pages/index.aspx
Learn about infectious diseases and the immune system.

http://www.pbs.org/newshour/globalhealth/archive.php?id=8
Read the latest on global health watch.

http://science.nationalgeographic.com/science/health-and-human-body/human-diseases
Information and photos relating to a variety of infectious diseases.

Index

Page numbers in **bold** refer to maps and photos.